Precious Moments with God
Volume One

Allen Ray

Precious Moments with God

Volume One

LARGE PRINT

In loving memory of

Frances Irene Stansell Ray.

Copyright © 2022 by Allen Ray

All rights reserved. No part of this book may be reproduced, scanned, or distributed in any printed or electronic form without permission. Please do not participate in or encourage piracy of copyrighted materials in violation of the authors rights. Purchase only authorized editions.

ISBN: 66395724R00037

BOOK DESIGN & PHOTOGRAPHY BY CAMERA WORKS

Forward

"…Test me in this," says the LORD Almighty, "and see if I will not throw open the floodgates of heaven and pour out so much blessing that there will not be room enough to store it."   Malachi 3:10 NIV

It all began with a big canvas tent in the middle of a field on Boone Ford Road in Gordon County. Inside the tent were rows and rows of metal chairs on a grass floor. An upright piano was positioned to one side of the homemade platform, and a pulpit stood in the middle. Many souls were saved as the wind slipped in and out of the fabric walls carrying the sound of singing and the preaching of the Word.

Not long after the tent revival, Billy Gene Quarles donated that field for the foundation of a house of the Lord. He was one of the founders of the new church, a charter member and eventually served as a Deacon.

Billy Gene's brother, Harold Quarles, was the founding pastor of the little country church in Calhoun, Georgia. Under the guidance of Reverend Harold Quarles, and after much prayer and planning by many who had attended the revival, Boone Ford Missionary Baptist Church was formed.

On a Sunday night, November 24, 1974, the Reverend Harold Quarles moderated a meeting of those congregated as the founding members of Boone Ford Missionary Baptist Church. By unanimous vote, he was elected by the assembled body to serve as pastor with the option to give a 30-day notice before leaving.

Following the election, a church conference was called into session, and the visitors were invited to remain in attendance. Next, was a call for peace and fellowship. All in attendance stood in agreement.

The doors of the church were opened for membership, and 31 people came forward to become the charter members of Boone Ford Missionary Baptist Church.

During a later Sunday evening service on January 19, 1975, the doors of the church were again opened for membership. A dozen folks came forward to join the church by letter, by statement, or as candidates for baptism. Among those were Allen and Frances Ray. Allen was joining by letter to transfer his membership from Salem Baptist Church and Frances was joining by letter to transfer her membership from West Union Baptist Church.

And so, the little country church grew in this same manner—with the doors opened wide and people joining by the dozens. The Spirit moved among this congregation. Many members discovered they had been blessed with different gifts. Allen Ray accepted his gift as writing down what was happening and how he felt during this time. Several others shared this same gift. This volume and the ones that follow are a window into a time of great passion for the Lord and great love for each other.

The floodgates of heaven had been opened and the blessings were poured out.

Vickie McEntire

Table of Contents

Testimony 1

My Vision 3

The Second Gift 7

The Four Christians 9

God's People 13

The Searcher 17

Unknown 21

The Greatest Blessings 23

Servants 29

Something Worth Living For 33

Hearts of Stone, Gold & Pure.........37

Satisfied Mind...............................39

Our Shadowed Sins......................41

Love is a Beautiful Thing 43

A Thought....................................45

Always God's Ways 51

Our Church 55

Harm Can Never Befall Us 57

Writer's Notes..............................59

Precious Moments with God
Volume One

I was glad when they said unto me, let us go into the house of the LORD. Psalm 122:1

Your best friend died and rose again for you.

Testimony

Jesus, Jesus, he died on the tree to save you and me from this cruel world of sin.

Halleluiah, praise his Holy Name.

I wandered away from God out into this world of sin, sorrow and shame.

Thinking I could make it on my own, but things never go better without God.

Oh, how true and wonderful He is.

Then one day, Jesus said, "It's about time for us to have a little talk about old times."

He stretched out his arms and said, "Come on back into the family you once left behind for those worldly goods."

And now, I'm so happy, glad and free since I'm back trying to live and do everything He says. When he calls me home now, I'll be ready to go, because it's a cold and lonely world down here below.

My Vision

When God first appeared to me one night, I thought it was just something of my imagination, but now I know differently. I don't understand why it was me or what for, but I have found out after rededicating my life to God

that there is no need to question anything God tells you, for He's always right. He has a purpose for each and every one of us here on earth.

Since the first message He gave me, I've never lingered or not written it down. I pray for understanding and guidance to know what to do with it, but I never doubt what, or who it's for. God already knows and sees that they get it. Since I've been writing these messages down, I have grown closer and closer to God. It seems as if He's right there in the room with me and talking to me and oh, what happiness I find each and every time. I could stand up and shout and praise His Holy Name.

Why, I even feel like preaching, but each time I talk it over with Him and I am sure now that it's not for me to preach, but to write these messages so as for someone else to read and understand more about His Holy Word and Him. My, He's so wonderful. I wish everyone knew Him as I do. For with Him, everything is possible. He said if we will seek, we will find; if we will ask, we shall have. I wouldn't trade my gift for anything or give it to anyone, for I know there is but one God and I know He's real.

The Second Gift

We go to church when we are lost, and when God's drawing power comes to us, we kneel at the altar and receive Jesus Christ as our Lord and Savior and go forth telling everyone we come in contact with—that we think are lost—of the wonderful feeling of being free and all our burdens and heavy loads lifted. But that's not all there is for some. They receive the Holy Spirit right then, but others sometimes don't receive it at the same time. I guess it's God's way of testing some of us to see if we are willing to take on duties of our Christian lives and not give up at the first sign of a stumbling block. It's not so hard to do God's will if we put all our trust and faith in God's hands and not only halfway. God will not take us on a sharing basis, but only on a full-time basis. It's wonderful to be a complete Christian. Praise the Lord.

The Four Christians

There is number one that never reads the Bible, nor says grace before meals, goes to church on Sunday for preaching only, just to be seen.

Then, there is number two, who never reads the Bible, except at church on Sunday for preaching, no Sunday School, but maybe occasionally Sunday night if something special is going on.

Then, there is number three, who reads his Bible occasionally, says grace sometimes, if the preacher is over for dinner. Goes to Sunday School sometimes, goes to preaching regularly, sings in the choir, helps in the church when needed, and is always ready to help anyone in need of help. He only thinks to pray when he is in trouble and there's no one else to turn to.

Then, there is number four, who reads his Bible daily and prays daily, says grace before each and every meal, attends church regularly, attends Sunday School every Sunday, sings in the choir, prays if called upon to. He helps in any way that he can testify for the Lord on his job or off, daily spreading the Word of God. Yes, this includes preachers, deacons, and church congregations.

Yes, we should stop and think about which one we are, that's right, if we need to be a better Christian, then let's get down and ask for God's help. If we think we don't need help and are living according to God's way, then let's help and pray for someone else who does. God will bless you for it.

God's People

There are two kinds of people on earth, the Christians and the sinners. We, the people of the devil, have everything—we think. We have money, the root of all evil. We have new cars, boats, new houses. And, anything we want here on earth to satisfy our earthly wants. We think we're above and better than everyone else. We don't need to go to church or need to know Jesus. We go fishing, or work on whatever arises on Sunday that we need to do. It's no different from any other day of the week to us.

We, the people of God, are the ones that have everything. It's not anything that's on earth or of man. We have Jesus, the most precious and loving Savior. For when we have a need, we only ask and we receive. We don't need money or any other worldly possession, for we are fed when we are hungry, and we have drink when we are thirsty. We don't have to worry about our problems or cares. We just turn them over to Jesus and He takes care of them always. We are too busy to worry about them. For we are working for the Master now. He's never slack or out of reach when we need Him. Oh, if those other people could only know Jesus and the wonderful life they could live. They wouldn't have to give up anything, just know the most important thing first and keep it first—Jesus.

Oh, the joy and peace and happiness we always have. That is, we Christians, we have that. That they can't steal or buy from anyone, but they can ask for it any time and receive it free. Thank you, dear Jesus, for making it possible for me to have it. What? Your Love.

The Searcher

He's the modern-day Christian that says, "I am never satisfied in this or that church. It's just not what I'm searching for." They're not looking for peace, joy and happiness. They're not looking for all those things. For, if they were true Christians, they would have found it in any humble and Spirit-seeking House of God. What they are really seeking is the true and honest down-to-earth repentance and salvation and the thorough cleansing of the soul and giving of their hearts to God. A lot of times we seem dissatisfied with ourselves because of something we think God has given us to do. We say we can't do it. But, did you ever stop and think about it? If it were something that God has told us to do, or maybe the devil has stepped in while we weren't looking and we got a little slack. It might not be what God wants us to do. Then is the time to really pray about it like you never prayed before.

If you have been truly saved by the Grace of God, you won't have any slack or open place for the devil to get close to you. When you really believe in the Lord, Jesus, He's all you should ever have on your mind. So, stop and look around you. That's right, what have they got that I don't have. That's right, the best way to find out is to stop the searching and kneel down and ask God. He will tell you and more than gladly give you your portion. That's right, this wonderful love. You never had it completely before. Ain't you glad you're traveling days are over?

Unknown

When He reached down for me, when God reached down His hand for me. I was sinking deep in sin and sorrow, when He reached down His hand for me.

I'm living now to see that home He has prepared for me. For some day, we all shall see it.

When He reached down for me, when God reached down His hand for me. I was sinking in sin and sorrow, when God reached down for me. When God reached down His hand for me, He brought me out and up to see the lights of that beautiful city.

When He reached down for me, when God reached down His hand for me. I was sinking in sin and sorrow, when He reached down His hand for me. Jesus saves. Jesus lasts forever. Jesus came and died for you and me. Jesus was tired, but Jesus never cried. Jesus only wept once, when His friend died. Jesus' side was pierced, Jesus then died. Now, Jesus is on God's side. Jesus said come. Jesus is always at home. Jesus now lives on that throne.

The Greatest Blessings

Now, when I need a blessing, all I have to do is to think Lord, Jesus. Then, they start to pouring out to me as long as I keep in touch with the Lord. Praise His Holy Name. Now, if you want to really be happy and all filled up and running over, just go to the place, any place, where the Spirit is at. Where two or three are gathered and are talking and rejoicing in my Lord's Name, where there's crying, shouting and some mighty big tears rolling down my cheeks, you know it is all there and happening. What? The most wonderful and precious moments when I'm talking to the Lord and praising Him for being such a wonderful God. He never changes. He's always the same, no matter if it has been ten minutes or ten years. His love is forever. Now, you take this special occasion coming up, oh, I can hardly wait until Sunday. Why? Because we are starting our revival and I know God has already started blessing His bearers of His Word, who are to take part in it. Oh, I pray each day for Him to be in each and every service nightly and to guide lost souls into His House that they might come under conviction and turn their lives over to Him before it's too late, and to go out into the world a new person and help others to find His love and grace. Oh, we have the most wonderful group of God's people in our small church. Why, if you were passing by sometime and heard us rejoicing, you would think you were in heaven. Oh, how wonderful God is to have sent Brother Harold, that it might be made possible through our precious Lord, to have this wonderful House of the Lord built, and built upon the Rock.

Then came Brother Walter, another wonderful man of God always testifying and teaching the most Holy and gracious Word of God. Oh, we are growing by leaps and bounds, in the will of God, helping to be a small light unto the straight and narrow path that leads to glory. Oh, how precious are the many, many wonderful blessings He has poured out upon us. We thank Thee, Lord, for ever and ever. Amen.

Lord, we thank Thee for whatever little part each day we have in carrying on the beautiful words of the Gospel. Lord, thou hast been so gracious to us Father, that we will never be able to repay only a small part of our debt. But, Lord, we will meet You in our home in glory, trying to pay the interest on the loan. Father, we thank You for Thy son, Bill, who gave us the land for the church. Father, why do we—when we're lost—think it's so hard to love Thee, when it's not? For, when we have Your love in our hearts and souls, we have love for everyone and cannot find out who our enemies are because of the overflowing cup of kindness thou have given us, never to run dry. For once you drink of the living waters, you never thirst again. Lord, it's so easy for one to give their life to Thee, but Lord, for me it was the hardest, longest walk down that short aisle to Your outstretched arms. Oh, I wish I had known when I was younger, where I could have lived for Thee most of my life. Now, Lord, I thank Thee for all these beautiful messages Thou gave to me, that might help but one lost soul to stop and think of You before it's too late.

Servants

We may be here today and gone tomorrow. Who knows what God has in store for us from day to day. We say the Lord has led us to go here or there to do this or that. That's all well and good, but He never says how long for any particular thing. Sometimes, we may try to stay and do things longer than God wants us to, which is wrong.

So, we shouldn't have to be told twice by the Lord when to go. Also, we may go before we should, not really waiting on the Lord to tell us. We get too anxious. Why am I writing this? Because the Lord told me to. I never doubt or hesitate when He speaks to me. I have before, but what I did, I did it on my own, not knowing until it was too late, that the Lord wasn't with me at the time of it. But, when it was over, He let me know that I tried it on my own and failed. Sometimes, we become discouraged and think God has forgotten us, but we are wrong, for He's always got something for us to do at the right place at the right time. If we try it on our own, we could be hurting someone instead of helping, because God had dealt with the other person, also. He knows when he should receive your message, not before, or too late, at the right time. The Lord works in mysterious ways. We don't always understand why, but when we fully put our trust in Him and obey Him, everything will be all right. We sometimes feel like the Lord has given us an awful small part to play. But, did you ever stop to think that even the smallest part may be the largest and most precious to the Lord? Maybe just going to church each and every time the doors are open and testifying for the Lord could do more for someone than a house full of preachers. So, our part is never too small.

Something Worth Living For

When we are children, we are taught about God and His Son, Jesus, when he was born and His early life. As we grow older, we are taught of Him being baptized by John and all the miracles He did while He was here on earth, all about His disciples and about the crucifixion of Jesus on the cross, and His being put in the tomb, only to be rise in three days waiting to ascend into heaven to be with His Father before coming back in Spirit to be with His disciples. And tell them of that glorious home awaiting them in heaven after their death. We never really took all this to heart until most of us were married or grown into adulthood. Then, we see and feel the wonderful blessing of the Holy Ghost. Oh, if we could have only understood all the beautiful things that are in the Bible. Oh, how wonderful it is to hear Christians testifying for the Lord. As we grow old, we come to love and cherish all these beautiful memories and also see how much closer to the Lord we have grown, and how much more we understand why we must live each and every day for God, and God only, not ourselves. Before, I could not wait until church was over to get out and do my thing; but now I feel so much sorrow and unhappiness when services are over and we have to go home. Why? I'd rather be in church 24 hours a day than to have all the riches of the world. Why? I just can't get enough of the promise of that heavenly home. Why? There's nothing on earth they say can even come close to being like it. Oh, when we see Jesus again, won't it be so wonderful, when all the worldly cares are left behind. Never again to hinder us as a stumbling block. We love one another now, but not like the love our Lord, Jesus Christ, has for us. It can never be compared to anything we call love. Oh, how wonderful it is to be able to go to church and worship in stillness and the Spirit as we see fit, and not have to worship as someone else tells us how to. My, to be able to have freedom of worship is the most wonderful gift that is taken for granted by many people. No one knows how much love another has for him until they are in a good old-fashioned fellowship service when nothing is there but you and them and most of all, God, and His love and kindness. Come and see sometime and I'll bet you'll be back the next time if you have the love of Jesus.

Hearts of Stone, Gold & Pure

There are hearts of stone, the ones who never want to even speak of Jesus or even the Bible. They don't have time or it bores them, because they think someone is trying to force something on them and it hardens their hearts. Then, there is the heart of gold, so to speak, he's willing to help anyone, anytime with any worldly goods. But he's never got time to worship God or even read His Word. But, one day after a while, it will be too late. Now, here is the most valuable one of them all: it's the one where he will do anything for you, night or day. Why? He's got something special for you they don't have. What? He can pray for you. That is worth more than anything else in the world. These are the ones that have happiness, joy and hope for tomorrow to see Jesus coming after them.

Satisfied Mind

I once was lost in sin when Jesus took me in. He sought me and bought me with His blood. He died on the cross that I might live and never die. He arose from the tomb to be in Spirit to watch over me and lead me down the path of righteousness and to guide me daily doing His will and learning more about the Bible and what it means to us Christians. Oh, how I love Jesus, how precious He is to me. I wish everyone knew Him; how beautiful it would be. There would be no fighting or quarreling or any unhappiness to live through daily. Jesus is a friend to the ones who know Him and will always care for you, no matter what. He holds all your burdens in His hands.

Our Shadowed Sins

Our shadowed sins are the ones we never realize or think about because they might be small or unnoticeable to us, but noticeable to others. They are where we might just get a little cross with someone or in a lightly heated argument. Nonetheless, they are as big as any sin in the sight of God. They don't prevent us from fellowshipping or worshipping God in Spirit and truth, but they're still there. Probably if we stopped and looked at all our sins, we wouldn't even be in church. But God doesn't work that way with His people. Our job is to do His will every day and He will take care of us. They are all around us, but God didn't make us totally perfect. There has only been one perfect human being to walk this earth. Jesus. So, you see, if we were perfect what each of us would have to live through each and every day.

Love is a Beautiful Thing

We love our neighbors, fathers and mothers, here on earth, that we know and see. But, do we love the most important One whom we physically cannot see, the Lord, Jesus? We never have doubts and sorrows when we are with Him every day. But did we ever stop to think about the most wonderful love Jesus gives to us each and every day? We can never return as much love in a lifetime as He gives us in a month or even a meeting where the Spirit is so strong it makes us shout. Oh, if we could only see and feel Him in these times, to hug and kiss Him and tell Him how much we love Him. God also loves us so much that He gave His only Son to die for us. Would we do the same? That's something to think about, ain't it.

A Thought

From dust we are made. God gave us a soul, heart and body with life. How precious it is, yet we cherish the things of the world and do not stop to think of our body, mind and spirit. We are so caught up in a world of ungodly things and places that we forget to pray and give thanks to God Almighty for His great blessings and favors He has seen fit to bestow upon us each and every day and night. We are but servants of the devil until we give our lives completely to God, to live each day in the straight and narrow way to heaven.

Down here on earth we should have but one God and praise God each and every day for His blessings and favors. He shall come again for us but will we be able to say Lord, I've done all I can for the glory of heaven and for my Father? And now, Lord, judge me not for the sins of others whom I have tried to help see the light and give their lives to You and to turn completely from sin and lust of all these worldly things.

Help us now, Lord, to walk that last mile without a sinful snare or the slightest temptation to return to the devil as a servant. Now, Lord, we thank You for all You have done for us, for guiding us and reaching down a helping hand when we call upon You. Oh, Jesus, we thank Thee and praise Thee for having died on the cross for us that it might be fulfilled that which was told our forefathers, that You would come again that we might have life and have it more abundantly.

We thank Thee for the peace and joy we now have and the blessings we receive in each and every service for Thee. Again, Lord, we ask Thee to help us on that last narrow stretch before we reach our home in glory. God is wonderful to us who know Him. He's worth more than all the silver and gold in the world to us. He abides with us always. No one can ever buy this love from you or me or anyone. It's free to anyone, rich or poor, for the asking. Makes no difference who you are, He loves you always.

I got down on my knees one day and talked it all over with Him, and now I know there's nothing else that can ever replace it in my life. For now, I live and praise Him. For now, I have a ray of hope, maybe just a small ray, but the more I live and praise God daily, the bigger it gets.

God has given each and every one of us a gift, the most gracious of them all—life eternal. He's always on the other end of the line. All we have to do is to call the right number. He's never too busy to talk to us no matter what time of night or day it is. He always has the answer to our problems if we will only look for them and trust and obey Him. I know, for He's never let me down. Now, my question to you is: Why hasn't anyone joined this wonderful family? They don't know what they're missing in life.

Always God's Ways

We sometimes think we should do this the way we want to, but we're always wrong. No matter how hard or easy, simple or complicated it might be, we should always obey God.

Sometimes it seems a little bit hard to tell the difference between what God wants us to do and what we think we want to do. During these times, it's best not to make quick judgements or decisions without praying about it until we are satisfied with an answer.

We think sometimes we can do something without first talking it over with God, and we make a mess out of things and then ask God to have His way.

Oh, if we would only trust and obey Him 24 hours a day, we wouldn't find ourselves in these fixes.

God is wonderful, though. He will never refuse to do anything for you that you ask. He's not like human beings, we do what we want to our own way. We are saved by His way, not by man's.

The preacher preaches God's way, not his way. The teachers teach God's way, not their way. The singers sing the way God wants them to. God never does anything that's not needed. No matter how difficult or simple it may be, there's a purpose for it.

Our Church

That's right, our church, God's and mine and yours. Well maybe not 50/50, but more like God's 99%. God's always there, but sometimes we're not. But God doesn't always punish us for being absent. We can never thank Him enough for what He has provided us with: the building, pastor and congregation.

In our church, everybody is the same. No one is better than his brethren or sister. Some churches you know have sections in them, so to speak, for different persons to sit. But we can thank God for what we have. Any and every one anytime would do anything for you night or day. That's a fact.

When you walk in the door, you can feel God's presence. We're all one big happy family. We never turn our noses up at anyone, no matter if we have never met you before. Try us.

Harm Can Never Befall Us

We oftentimes blame God for things that didn't work out the way we wanted them to or something that we prayed about that didn't come to pass. But did we ever stop and think about it and study about it after it was all over with and see really whose fault it was? That's right, it's always ours, because we didn't really totally put it in God's hands. He never refuses to answer prayers, but does things in His own way and timing. Maybe He wants us to take a look at ourselves before we start asking favors and blessings. Maybe we need to do something about our lives, instead of asking Him to help someone else.

    He knows what we need and when we need it. So, we don't need to jump to conclusions or blame God for something that's our fault.

Writer's Notes

These words you have just read come from God, the Almighty. None are mine. I have only had a small part in this and that is receiving and writing them down as He gave them to me. So, the Author of these poems is God; the writer is me. They never get old or not interesting to me. For I'll cherish them always as a most precious gift from God, my Father. Thank you, Lord. Praises be to You always and may I ever be in Thy will. Amen.

                                    Allen Ray